Barefoot

Piotr Florczyk

Barefoot

20/20 **EYEWEAR**
PAMPHLET SERIES
2015

First published in 2015 by Eyewear Publishing Ltd
74 Leith Mansions, Grantully Road
London W9 1LJ United Kingdom

Typeset with graphic design by Edwin Smet
Author photograph by Dena Florczyk
Printed in England by Lightning Source
All rights reserved © 2015 Piotr Florczyk

The right of Piotr Florczyk to be identified as author of this work has been asserted in accordance with section 77 of the Copyright, Designs and Patents Act 1988

ISBN 978-1-908998-67-5
WWW.EYEWEARPUBLISHING.COM

Thanks

I am deeply grateful to many people for their kindness and support of this work, especially my mentor Sandra Alcosser, Veronica Andrew, Robin Davidson, Boris Dralyuk, Ilya Kaminsky, David Shook, Susan Stewart and Kevin Wisniewski.

Special thanks to Todd Swift and the entire Eyewear crew for guiding this pamphlet into the world.

for my family and friends

Table of contents

- 9   Barefoot
- 10   Omaha Beach
- 11   Salt
- 13   Tetris
- 15   Lullaby
- 16   The Bazaar
- 17   The Chess Players
- 18   Stoppage Time
- 19   Camera Obscura
- 20   Pastoral
- 21   Room for Rent
- 23   Bric-a-Brac
- 24   Fairway Falls
- 25   Birthday Party
- 27   Fieldwork
- 28   Homeland Security
- 29   Ink
- 32   The Grid
- 33   Moving Sale
- 34   Psalm

Barefoot

A Monday like any other, with shadows
and lights united in speechless collage—

while barefoot I go down
the twenty concrete steps

to pick up the paper from under
a palm tree with a hair-sprayed crown

and it's now I suddenly remember,
unsure why, the creased

voices of Mother and Father
asking me not to forget

to take off my shoes and feel the cold ground
in every place I'd like to call *Home*

Omaha Beach

Returning here, it hasn't been easy
for them to find their place in the black sand—
always too much sun or rain,
strangers driving umbrellas yet deeper

into their land. The young radio host said so,
speaking of the vets. When the sea had come,
some curled up inside the shells;
others flexed and clicked their knuckles

on the trigger of each wave, forgetting
to come up for breath. Then, as now, there was
no such a thing as fin-clapping fish,
quipped the host—his voice no more than

an umlaut going off the air. But he didn't
give us a name at the start or the end.
Nor did he explain how to rebury a pair of
big toes jutting out from the mud

at the water's edge. In the end, it's a fluke.
A beach ball gets lost. And a search
party leads us under the pier, into the frothy sea
impaling empty bottles on the rocks.

Salt

Breathless, the visitors
bow and stream
single file into the tunnel,
kept alive by the ribs
of trestles creaking above.

The guide turns on his headlamp.

After eight hundred years
the walls feel rough
under a hand.
The air's cold
with smell engineered
by dynamite, picks, and spades.

The first chamber was dug in the name
of her Majesty's love of salt;
soon more followed to pay
for the Battles of Grunwald,
Vienna, and Somme.

Today pensioners lean
against the velvet rope,
photographing themselves
with a heap of broken ladders.

The teens finger "Alice Was Here"
spray-painted on the steel door.

At a quarter-mile below the surface,
the miners had laid the rails,
pushed the wheelbarrows,

loaded the carts.
Stood no chance.

They shared each pocket of air,
then froze in the flash
of methane,
or bit the flood's muddy tongue.

While their mules ran wild,
the lucky ones clung to stalactites
teething overhead.

Eventually, people learned
how to carve a bowl-shaped
concert hall around the mass graves.
They hold weddings here.

The gargoyles crack more each day.

"Until they break off and scatter
around these cobbled floors,
we'll kindle the dust," says the guide,
turning off his lamp.

"Our safety record is spotless."

"Now take this lantern,
hold it high over your head,
and follow the signs
to the lake, coppery in color and taste.
There a young guide
will meet you and take you upstairs."

Whatever you think,
do not imagine that you're leaving
empty-handed.

Tetris

While searching for a place to eat our sandwiches
of honey ham, Swiss cheese, we came to the edge of

a tract I once lived in, unsure why I had left,
unsure why thistles grew where a bike path had been,

and leaving you to guard the gate, I went inside
a five-story block, pretending I didn't know the way.

But the staircase remembered my stride—its wooden
planks creaked and squeaked as I climbed slowly, holding on

to the wrought-iron rail. The air was thick with flies,
the smell of fresh tar sizzling on the roof, where,

years ago, we'd go to spit on people's heads and tweak
the antennas to catch somebody else's dreams.

Life was beautiful, I thought, leaving the first floor.
I found my misspelled nickname carved into the wall.

The second story, too, held a secret I would never
forget. The teenage years. Boys chasing girls.

The painted-shut window with the view of the church.
The hollow spot under the stairs where she told me

I had to take my clothes off before she would hers.
(After she unplugged the extension cord, the light-

bulb that dangled above went out, shivering stars
around us.) Out of breath, I pushed on.

Arriving on the third story, I wondered what
became of Peter and Paul. They started shaving

in junior high, grew to be six-foot-four. I'd heard
they followed the dusty footprints their father left

coming home at night, and got a job underground.
Who knows, they might well be in Dublin or Belfast,

tossing back pints in an empty pub. No wonder
the fourth floor was a blur, and the fifth why I came.

But when I rapped my white knuckles on the door,
the brownish leatherette cover caved in under

my wedding ring. So I checked the address again—
apartment 9, last building on the right, dead end

street lined with lilacs—*check*, *check*, *check*, I flipped
through memories, hoping to see the familiar eye

plug the Judas hole, hear the turning of the locks,
the clinking of the chain lifted and unhooked, dropped.

Lullaby

Wrapped in sheets like a mummy, or a wound, you can tell
      it is not a murmur
but something lesser still that you hear when you eavesdrop
      on the couple

having sex next door. Their bodies, gasping and changing gears,
      are in the way—
stuck between you and some muffled yelp that travels down
      the dimpled walls.

If only they stopped ringing the doorbell, those tipsy carolers,
      maybe you could
finally hear the conch in your head. Insured by Smith & Wesson,
      powered by

Rita's Apple Pie, you won't catch any Zs tonight, since the footsteps
      and toilet flush
give way to MAYDAY being tapped on the pipe above.
      Is fire alarm next in line?

You've fed the dying goldfish, paid the gas bill… And now you put
      your lips on
your wife's open mouth, sorry to see it adrift on the pillow,
      like an island in high seas.

The Bazaar

Because we couldn't lose him, we tried
again and again, diving into alleys, between

and behind rows of cots and makeshift stalls
piled high with smoked herring, sabers and porn.

He had every corner covered, and greeted us
with a sausage boa around his neck

or flashing a knocked-off brand-name purse.
For this was the place to renegotiate

ourselves, he said, as we once were.
To buy a soul, learn the official language

spoken nowhere else, exchange our American
dollars for a fine-toothed master key

that unwinds the most stubborn of clocks.
And so we kept running, while he

kept raising his arm in protest like a referee.
Still, before we gave up on finding our dead,

we stumbled upon a double-masted
schooner stuck in an old vodka bottle

anchored in mud, and we imagined boarding it,
then saw people waving and calling across

the lapping waves to each other, and while seeing
we heard at last the faint echo they left leaving.

The Chess Players

Glued to the metal stools
they contemplate the next move,
hiding their faces
in their hands. They say,

Make up your mind,
Franz, you've got a medal
for shooting down Reds.
Come on now, Mick,

you've served worse
than queens and kings.
To keep track of time,
they pass a paper bag around.

When a nosy robin breaks
into song, they unbutton their shirts
and feel their broomstick backs.
At least one of them

has lost a leg riding trains—
somewhere—another pushes
a squeaky stroller
uphill.

Stoppage Time

I'm not sure how soccer
explains the world,
though books
are written about that, you know.

If the ball sneaks in, grazing
the post and the crossbar,
the upper-ninety
shot doesn't take us

into a bedroom,
where a TV's always on.
Democracy means everyone
gets to play—

regardless of who rules
the clock or the stands—
like in baseball:
our turn, their turn…

In another place, you
know, that fucker,
grabbing his shin and faking
a foul, would be our friend.

Camera Obscura

Once upon a time, I also took pictures
that could speak for themselves.
Are these photoshoped?
The black-and-white hurts
though not enough to make me squint or cry
at the sight of what's gone.
Look, the slaves are long dead;
the coal mined by those stickmen burns on
in our atmosphere.
As for the sailors reeling in
the panicked sails on a Saturday
near Dana Point, well,
the photographer got his shot
and they were never seen or heard from again.

That's all I've got to say
about recreating the past from scratch.
The women with children
clutching their rag dolls and teddy bears—
they're here to escape the heat.
But the junkyard's beautiful—
don't you think so?
Row after row of droopy headlights
and toothless bumpers.
"Will you be my Valentine?"
You can have your pick of year and make.
And on clear days, when the cranes hoist the wrecks up,
see the breeze nudge their wheels
to turn back.

Pastoral

I was born in a city—you've never been there. I rubbed shoulders
    with buildings, blue
trams, and pigeons. Then I had this idea to take a hike and get
    some fresh air elsewhere.

The idea wasn't mine, but nor were the oaks I hugged with strangers,
    or the lashing
brook I stood in barefoot, catch-and-releasing. I followed the rules
    and stayed on the trail.

Then I changed my mind, decided to leave, but couldn't find
    my way back. The idea
was mine. I've carried it around like a breadcrumb; neighbors think
    I've got stuff

up my sleeve. So we're learning together how to cross an intersection
    with the lights
turned off, or how to tell a real turnip from a knockoff. No one
    complains if, out of

boredom, I slingshot rocks at their windows, but when I stagger
    with a story of the sun
climbing a fire escape in the rain, they ask not for the ending but
    for silence, something

like a furrow or a dagger.

Room for Rent

Carpeted, the room is
small, smaller than nothing.
Up on cinder blocks,
the twin bed
juts out like a sore thumb,
hardly leaving any space for
the desk and chair.

But the silence is misleading.
Kept alive by a yellow tack,
Madonna rocks on
the far wall, next to
the map of the world.
In its center, a spider
devours its succulent prey.

Not far from here,
where Grant meets Pier,
the sparkling canal
carries dead bodies out to sea.
You can choose
to look the other way.
The rent is due on the first.

Are you religious?
We have a brand-new church,
but many prefer the tavern.
I promise not to intrude—
you can set the boxes down.
Starting over is about the walls
staring at each other.

Can you hear the sun
slicing the loaves of clouds?
The ellipsis
of scratches and dings
means love and grief are following
you here, are following
each other.

Bric-a-Brac

The second I turned away, he was playing with fire by smashing
    one red brick
after another, first against the shoulder-high wall he built, then
    against his forehead,

sunburned and creased beyond his years. Yet all morning nothing
    spelled that the end
was near. While he worked on encircling the eye of the well, calm
    as the level, I sat

in the ditch by the road, tapping a stick on the stump of the elm.
    Milk trucks went by.
I saw a hawk, and bald hens scuttling for cover. The well was just
    a hole in the ground.

But things began to unravel. Straightening up, my father looked
    down the shaft,
and saw his face like a cloud at the bottom. That's when the chain
    twirled, the water

changed color—he later claimed—it wasn't the way to go, not then,
    not ever. So he went
after the bricks and the well, spooked he wouldn't be there
    when the bucket came up.

Fairway Falls

The generator kicks in, coughing smoke signals over the retirement
    home, beyond
the eighteenth hole. There, men armed with thermoses tie themselves
    to the scaffolds,

then raise and drop their hammers, quietly chatting in Spanish.
    The seniors don't mind
the din, it seems. Some stretch on the grass among dandelions;
    others paint the sun

scaling the brown slopes. When the blonde nurse appears with a tray
    of earplugs,
they shrug in chorus, saying they've heard it all before. Like
    a week ago, when two golf carts

crashed into the bingo hall while a gal who's sixty-four gave birth
    to a healthy baby boy.
They've made peace with the men mending the view. Moved by nothing
    but the past,

they roam along the alleys. Guitar lessons, anyone? Drawn to its
    blood-shot lights,
some tried to climb the cell phone tower one night. Risking rapture
    now in the face of

something new, four of them are heading down across the bunker—
    moons of silver hair
against the trees. At the pond eyelashed with reeds, they drop
    to their knees, and drink.

Birthday Party

Not everyone who shows up on time knows your name by heart. A few
    are overdressed,
manicured, and want to debate how it feels to be halfway done,
    on your way to hell or

some other place without a zip code. Yet you recognize A., who sold
    you the first porn,
and K. who cried on your shoulder about being in love. Others
    ring the bell because of

their dimpled cheeks or perky breasts. There's nothing strange in her
    clinging to a bottle
of vodka, or him, leaning against the piano, pulling tighter and
    tighter on his white-and-

red polka dot tie. Since your heroes were hooded and carried away
    on flatbed trucks,
you've learned to live with furniture missing legs, how to find
    friends by whistling the

tunes your forefathers sang charging tanks with bayonets. But that's
    an old story, no
longer true. So when the street lamp outside comes on, and there's
    no more finger food

for fingers to find, you cut the white chocolate cake into squares
    for little Z., who now
sports a beard, and for G. who rode a mule across valleys and peaks
    with a Hallmark card

he could have sent priority. Meanwhile the present pile grows taller.
    D.'s in charge.
You love the way she places each box atop another, brushing against
    the columns just to

crown one with a basket of citrus soap bars. She's a keeper. Who else
    could order the rest
of one's life from inside this labyrinth, then not miss a beat when
    the band strikes up

a jaunty tune and the guests huddle like pebbles in a bowl or roses
    in a vase—the vessel
you stare into, searching for fallen thorns, while everyone wants to
    know if you'd rather

open the signed or unsigned gifts first.

Fieldwork

While I sit in my study, imagining
the way they cut you open at the neck
with glimmering scalpels, slid inside
to file down the spurred vertebrae,
extract two bulging discs—the workers

are already waist-deep in the hole,
scraping the rocks with shovels and picks
down the street. Not a small job
on this scorching day to drain the puddle
of muddy sewage, mend the pipes.

Not a small delight for me, either,
to watch how the one in torn denim shorts,
standing like a stamen abloom
in the crater, molds the sludge into
a statuette of himself—as I wish we too

were less ashamed of what lies hidden.
So, without clicking your tongue,
tell me about the moment
the surgeon's voice became the sound
of footsteps on frost. Hurry. Those men

will soon bring in the mixers and pour
concrete over the wound. Divide the street
with white cursors the size of stitches.
Hurry. The gurgling in the wall
means the water's coming back on.

Homeland Security

Somewhere in America, at a garden stand,
a hundred gnomes offer to hide a hundred keys.

Ink

How much did it cost me?
More than a hundred bucks
behind the multiplex—
and ulcers, gray hair.
But I had no choice: this deal
was the only one that made sense.
We shook on it.

And he handed me a box
marked *Toys for Tots* on the sides,
insisting I'd better not inspect
anything. He swore
the manual was included.
I paid him in cash
rolled up inside a fountain pen.

While he sped off
in a painter's white van,
I counted to twenty, as ordered,
and played hacky sack
with a Pepsi can.
Then I ran home, punching holes
in the walls along the way.

After I slipped unnoticed
into the house, beads of sweat
streaked down my face.
I let the printer rest
in the company of paperclips
on my Ikea desk;
it was heavier than I'd imagined.

For every button I understood,
there were many others
that baffled me, and levers
that moaned like cellos.
I got my middle finger stuck
in the paper tray,
trying to reach deep down.

At last stirred by feeling
rather than fate or fact,
I opened it up and planted a flag
of cyan, magenta, yellow and black
in its heart.
Gently, I slid
five hundred sheets inside.

The goal was to add up again
the correspondence
I'd carried on with myself,
the maple out front,
and my wife's amber eyes—
the way they trapped my lies.
For if there was a chance

to redeem myself, this was it.
While I was shaking out
my whites at the laundromat
when we first met,
the painter said he thought of art
as windows and doors.
So I pressed PRINT

and stopped the maple
from shedding leaves.
To my wife in the next room,

bundled up like a burrito
on that cold night,
I promised not a waiting room
of dimmed lights, but a life.

The Grid

At 6 a.m., the freeway enters my house with squeaking brakes
    and diesel fumes.
Three kids stuck in the backseat kick me in the shins. I toss
    and turn

until my body loses its edges, rolls off the bed and into
    the bathroom,
where I shave to exchange one face for another. Engines, engines
    everywhere.

It's not the exhaust that kills me, only the ricocheting sound
    of tires
jumping the fissures. The rosary of cars tooting their horns
    as though

only a few were allowed safe passage. Swerve and swear.
    Speed and spoil.
By 8 the 405 idles in my living room, the headlights go out.
    I am the overpass;

I wish I were the Exit.

Moving Sale

Down past the Food Giant and the Sunoco,
a bouncy castle rocks besieged by bungalows.
Like a medusa, the crowd takes on the shape
of smoke, snacking on grilled chicken and dogs.
There's a stroller whose wheel just rolled off;
a Tonka fire truck salvaged from a fire.
Empty picture frames and chrome-plated stools
cast a shadow on LPs finding their groove.
"Buy any button, get one engraved
with your name"—a sign on the fence.
Stacked in a dish rack, a romantic dinner set
defines what some men do for other men.
When a jogger drips sweat onto a plate, knife
and fork, he licks them clean before running off.

Psalm

When you visit
again, Lord, please
take everything

that is not here
to stay, to be
long after me.

See, all my junk
has been sorted,
scooped and neatly

stacked in three piles
against the wall.
This stained futon,

this wobbly chair
and the coffee
table, can be

carried at once
upon your back.
All the tools of

my crime are here,
packed in the wood
box sealed and nailed

shut for the road.
Read the labels—
not in Coptic,

Aramaic,
but in plain speech
of zeros, ones—

it will help You
decipher my
notes, thoughts, even

some bars of rage
written at night
in the margins

of books, white sheets
that my lovers
never found soft.

You see, I read
somewhere that we
are nothing but

fertilizer
for History, for
what's yet to come.

How funny then
that I now sit
leaning, blocking

my exit door.
Will you knock three
times, ring the bell?

Until you come,
pardon my dust,
my paper hat,

the fact that I,
dear Lord, kill time
tasting the hard

candy of your
body trembling
inside my mouth.

Acknowledgements

Grateful acknowledgement is made to
the editors of the publications in which some of the poems
or versions of the poems first appeared:
*Charlotte: A Journal of Literature and Art, Cimarron Review,
Gargoyle Magazine, The Laurel Review, The Literary Review,
The Louisville Review, The News Journal, New Orleans Review,
Notre Dame Review, Slate, The Southern Review,
The Yellow Nib.*

EYEWEAR PUBLISHING

EYEWEAR PAMPHLET SERIES

BEN STAINTON EDIBLES
MEL PRYOR DRAWN ON WATER
MICHAEL BROWN UNDERSONG
MATT HOWARD THE ORGAN BOX
RACHAEL M NICHOLAS SOMEWHERE NEAR IN THE DARK
BETH TICHBORNE HUNGRY FOR AIR
GALE BURNS OPAL EYE
PIOTR FLORCZYK BAREFOOT
LEILANIE STEWART A MODEL ARCHAEOLOGIST
SHELLEY ROCHE-JACQUES RIPENING DARK
SAMANTHA JACKSON SMALL CRIES

EYEWEAR POETRY

MORGAN HARLOW MIDWEST RITUAL BURNING
KATE NOAKES CAPE TOWN
RICHARD LAMBERT NIGHT JOURNEY
SIMON JARVIS EIGHTEEN POEMS
ELSPETH SMITH DANGEROUS CAKES
CALEB KLACES BOTTLED AIR
GEORGE ELLIOTT CLARKE ILLICIT SONNETS
HANS VAN DE WAARSENBURG THE PAST IS NEVER DEAD
DAVID SHOOK OUR OBSIDIAN TONGUES
BARBARA MARSH TO THE BONEYARD
MARIELA GRIFFOR THE PSYCHIATRIST
DON SHARE UNION
SHEILA HILLIER HOTEL MOONMILK
FLOYD SKLOOT CLOSE READING
PENNY BOXALL SHIP OF THE LINE
MANDY KAHN MATH, HEAVEN, TIME
MARION MCCREADY TREE LANGUAGE
RUFO QUINTAVALLE WEATHER DERIVATIVES
SJ FOWLER THE ROTTWEILER'S GUIDE TO THE DOG OWNER
TEDI LÓPEZ MILLS DEATH ON RUA AUGUSTA
AGNIESZKA STUDZINSKA WHAT THINGS ARE
JEMMA BORG THE ILLUMINATED WORLD
KEIRAN GODDARD FOR THE CHORUS
COLETTE SENSIER SKINLESS
ANDREW SHIELDS THOMAS HARDY LISTENS TO LOUIS ARMSTRONG
JAN OWEN THE OFFHAND ANGEL
A.K. BLAKEMORE HUMBERT SUMMER
SEAN SINGER HONEY & SMOKE
RUTH STACEY ALL THE LONG GONE QUEENS
BENNO BARNARD A PUBLIC WOMAN
HESTER KNIBBE HUNGERPOTS

EYEWEAR PROSE

SUMIA SUKKAR THE BOY FROM ALEPPO WHO PAINTED THE WAR
ALFRED CORN MIRANDA'S BOOK

EYEWEAR LITERARY CRITICISM

MARK FORD THIS DIALOGUE OF ONE

Printed by Libri Plureos GmbH in Hamburg, Germany